WINDWARD

Saint Julian Press

Poetry

"For those who can love - all at once - the words of Homer, of Sappho, of English renaissance verse and of Shakespeare, of Cavafy, of Seferis, of some anonymous woman whose singing of unrequited love is accidentally overheard by a passerby in some remote Greek village, the poetry of Kevin McGrath will bring unforgettable delight to both the heart and the mind." ~ Gregory Nagy

Francis Jones Professor of Classical Greek Literature and Professor of Comparative Literature and Director of the Center for Hellenic Studies at Harvard University

"Kevin McGrath is a rare poet of penetrating vision, attentive always to the ebb and flow of life, to beginnings, turnings, and endings, to the meeting places of sea and land, shore and horizon, to the thin and translucent places where light shines through the worlds of nature. His words bring love and light to days and nights, seasons and years, birth and death." ~ Diana Eck

Professor of Comparative Religion and Indian Studies, Master of Lowell House, and Director of the Pluralism Project at Harvard University

Windward

Poems

by

Kevin McGrath

Saint Julian Press
Houston

Published by
SAINT JULIAN PRESS, Inc.
2053 Cortlandt, Suite 200
Houston, Texas 77008

www.saintjulianpress.com

COPYRIGHT © 2015
TWO THOUSAND AND FIFTEEN
©Kevin MCGRATH

ISBN-13: 978-0-9965231-2-7
ISBN: 099652312X
Library of Congress Control Number: 2015945934

Cover art is an image of *Buddhaghosa Visits Suvarna Bhumi*,
Myanmar, 19th C., photo credit, Lilian Handlin.
Author photo credit Akos Szilvasi.

CONTENTS

ONE ... 1

TWO ... 3

THREE ... 6

FOUR ... 8

FIVE ... 11

SIX ... 15

SEVEN ... 18

EIGHT ... 21

NINE ... 23

TEN ... 25

ELEVEN ... 27

TWELVE ... 32

THIRTEEN ... 35

FOURTEEN ... 38

FIFTEEN ... 41

SIXTEEN ... 45

SEVENTEEN ... 49

EIGHTEEN ... 52

NINETEEN ... 54

TWENTY ... 56

TWENTY-ONE ... 59

TWENTY-TWO ... 61

TWENTY-THREE ... 64

TWENTY-FOUR ... 66

TWENTY-FIVE ... 69

TWENTY-SIX ... 74

TWENTY-SEVEN ... 76

TWENTY-EIGHT ... 79

TWENTY-NINE ... 81

THIRTY ... 83

THIRTY-ONE ... 85

THIRTY-TWO ... 87

THIRTY-THREE ... 89

THIRTY-FOUR ... 93

THIRTY-FIVE ... 96

THIRTY-SIX ... 100

A
VOYAGE
TOWARD THE NEW
WORLD DISCOVERY
VINE LAND
MAYFLOWER COLUMBINE
& CORN
BY INHERITANCE
INVITATION
GUIDE OUR VESSEL
O LADY OF PILOTS
TO NAVIGATE
IS NECESSARY
NOT TO LIVE

To Leanna

*Un punto solo m'è maggior letargo
che venticinque secoli a la 'mpresa
che fé Nettuno ammirar l'ombra d'Argo.*

Par. XXXIII, 96

WINDWARD

ONE

Now that the light is closing
And the circumference of days
Decreases and diminishes as
Darkness moves about
And we walk the years:

What grain do we leave behind
Heaped on a thin dry earth,
Offering what to the future
So others might enjoy more life,
Those who gave us laughter?

The old voice of human suffering
Whispering for centuries,
The sorrow that overcomes us
All our joy in loving and
Songs of marriage and birth:

Dust and sand and emptiness
A rainless dry cold world,
For night is the final condition
Of humanity and its going
Until we learn to be quite still.

From lakes and channels we arrived
Beached upon this world,
Beneath an arid rainfall
We drove our vessel shoreward
Pleasurably speechless:

To where the sea refounds
Its source and roads are home,
Going back perpetually
Truly aquiline in spirit -
Where consciousness began.

~WINDWARD~

We had built ourselves a ship
A boat that was unseen,
So beautiful that none perceived
How it flowed and how
Perfectly it moved the sea,
Attuned to a slow tempo
Of waves and full ocean:

Where a bird became a fish
A girl turned to a tree,
Irresistible as streams
Young men moved like water,
Silent as a gliding hawk
Crossing from limb to limb.

A bird rises from a stone
A fish vanishes in light,
A girl strips off her leaves
To reveal perfect form,
Or a young man insists
That his love is right and
Liberation a natural moment.

So launch your vessel soon
We are conceived at sea,
Repetition day by day
Where nothing is exclusive,
Send that ship on voyages
That none can ever say,
True wealth is never spoken.

TWO

A LIONESS in a tree
Gold among viridian,
Glittering like fire
Immutable and strong
Awaiting the right moment:

Or a soul with vermilion wings
Hovering on nets of life,
Tentative in its descent
Coming down to autumn earth
Marvellous with beauty.

The ebb and flow of ocean
Like the perfect moves of love,
Or birds crossing in the air
Floating on a light current
Mesmeric with suspense.

Slightly do the birds call
Experiencing no grief,
Their voices like zinc beads
Falling through dense air
Onto a copper-glittering lake.

Days come with long thin arms
Rays from the sun encircle
Reach out toward our sleep,
Words enter on our palate
We change and are remade.

Lion, bird, human ghost
Halt and are lost,
We observe the moment briefly
Unaware that the going
Is without effect.

Filled with earth's charisma
We walked down to the sea,
Toward a point where bare rocks
Rose above a frigid tide
With shadow curling in a wave.

~ WINDWARD ~

Two eagles were fishing there
Circling and prowling slowly,
We could hear the rush of air
As wide brown wings passed.

Stripping off our clothes we dived
Swam the gelid water
Far offshore in waves alone
Undisclosed from daily life.

The beauty of that moment
Was greater than the human,
Yet we cannot remember
What it was that occurred.

Yes - it was so and wonderful
Perfectly complete and good,
Immaculate without being
Able to recall itself:

Without acumen or vision and
Without the art we practice,
Without the deer and stones
Pines, spruce, birch or aspen:

A transfer of the sensible
Or code we might use,
Dance of bees or voice of crows
Migration of a humming-bird.

Is the supernatural
Guarding and protecting us,
Offering love a natural grace
To assist us in our going?

Invisible and inhuman
Without the javelins of time,
Without the lucid solar film
Which we wear upon our souls:

~ WINDWARD ~

Those leonine days stand about
With ductile voice, unblinking eyes,
Can they sing of only beauty
Of the love that made us know
How we are the more-than-human?

Their mobility of songs transmit
Phenomenal and streamlined night,
Whose ardent promises create
Lust to requite warm bodies,
Can we exist without their vision?

Life is slow and yet so brief
We rest scarcely in wandering,
Crossed by chains and threads we are
Woven in strange texts of love
Of taut fluency.

The underlying tunes we know
A music of no melody,
How is it we come and go
Unaware of their footfall
And thorough pace of years?

Leonine days gather close
Formed of cloudy shadow,
Scarlet jaws and salty breath
Where the sky groans and water sends
Slow perfumed humid showers:
The lions enjoy the passive earth
Wanting to take our spirit home.

THREE

GOODNIGHT summer, too long
Have you been about our walls,
Swallows have departed and
Acorns shower the fields,
Indestructible – your manner
Like a river between two stones
Runs away in darkness.

No one moves like you
Going throughout the world,
Singular and never plural
Beautiful with slow passage,
Queenly in gorgeous tones
Vivid with hollow cavities -
You figure of complete life.

We have walked incessantly
Your sensuous universal
Hundred-thousand years of kind,
Seen the looms on which
You dress our nude skin,
Our weak gentility exposed
Without your new clothing.

So many boats pass by
With flags, sails, and oars
Flashing with your high zenith,
Where now – but to be withheld
Within a broad stone cup
Upon your milky hands
As if we were libation:

Where we are reaped
Our veil stripped and
Undividingly we stand revealed,
Made to appease your ancestors
As we are poured upon
Your lakes, ponds, and islands
Where children play in shallows.

~Windward~

Horses amid brown shadowy oaks
Deer hidden beneath the wheat,
A fox upon cool fine sand
Among the bitter pines,
Within a curve of fern, partridge
Sleep as if never wakening
Even when the sun is raving.

Both seminal and fruitful
Running down-stream always
Messenger of the ideal Lost,
Goodnight summer for now
We harvest your gaunt leaves,
Your currency in this light world
All you gave us to renew.

Nothing can be lost by you
Nor can it be made strict
As this life evaporates within
Your coppery cadmium rays,
Tall monumental carmine clouds
From which you barely offer
To our thirst fresh rain
Coursing down across our shoulders.

The rock-walls of your altar
Now shine within a rising dusk,
Bats, owls, small quadrupeds
Commence a quiet patrol
In a sweetness of powdery air,
Where stars unbind our destiny
Reminding us of absolution.

For beauty once received
Cannot be retained
Is only ever ephemeral,
Your vision bears just one emotion
Sorrow that such visible good
Is not acquired by devotion
Cannot ever be recalled,
So, goodnight dear summer.

FOUR

The four winds about the world
That move within a human psyche,
First, the strange attraction going
Between male and feminine.

The second takes us on in time
So that we might look back
To residence and procession
Of what was lost upon our way.

The third is the emptiness
Filling up our breathing hours,
And as we go toward our source
Its quietness makes us more still.

The final air is that of beauty
Ephemeral, quick, and true,
The breeze that makes substantial
Everything we cannot prove,
Song of what we do not know.

A hare ran under a rainbow
Swallows flew throughout the rain,
Experience can be in seconds or
Even minutes and sometimes
We simply endure the years.

Racing through a wet forest
Across moss and standing pools,
Time or life and desire
Evade all captivity
Leaving neither scent nor trace.

We cannot see our freedom
Without grey or dark it lives,
Until our moral eye suddenly
Perceives the one fortune
We had assumed so long ago.

~ WINDWARD ~

Then walking down a sandy road
Suddenly it moved again,
Passing lightly before us
To swiftly enter in the woods
Soundlessly and printless.

Mist soon settled from offshore
The yellow stone on the coast
Became wet and gleaming,
A foghorn moaned to ships
The rainbow had vanished.

Was there a hare in the cedars
Living in solitary joy,
Or had we been mistaken
And nothing passed before us,
The long spare empty track
Revealed no sign of movement?

Yet without passion or volition
Horns curving and recurving,
Shadow glanced within the forest
By waterfalls and pools of silver:

A deer among cold rocks
Crossed by light and trees,
The motion of a mind toward
Absent things by inclination.

Green cliffs of slate and granite
Hemlock, pine, and balsam fir,
Where hawk and buzzard circled
Observing this abounding life.

Like opening and closing years
Optimism and its courage,
A vivid fiery youthfulness
Surrounded by so much dark:

~ WINDWARD ~

Waves of slow lightness roll
Upon bare mountain summits,
Broken stony ridges where
Quiet unspeaking beings stay:

Creative and enduring and
Unconscious of the winds' going,
Establishing a scheme of truth
Which the timing of a second
Momentarily betrays.

FIVE

In true vision we cannot
Close the eyes and only
The eyebrows move showing
How wonderful is the view.

Long green shade and fair grass
Embroidery of light on birches,
Willows reflecting off a lake
Where metalled water still retains
The carrion of aging night.

Mountain, forest, eagle, deer
Woodcock scattering in the bracken,
What is moving in our days
Has no inflection for our soul.

Look around the flame and say
What it is you see,
Desperation knows no word
Anguish has no dwelling.

Desertion eludes us for
Suddenly there is nowhere,
The future is elusive and
Its footprints indiscernible.

Unfamiliar and unknown
Being what we cannot say,
The sovereigns who lead us on
Walk unaware of progeny.

Both male and feminine they
Are never disappearing only
Changing how it is they speak,
Their chains are not conspicuous.

They move upon clairvoyant ways
Inviting and encouraging
As we approach their frontier
Announcing our experience, saying:

'Many times have we found
Peace beside you in the night,
Your smooth warm bones and
The perfect tempo that we love.

Falling into sleep so lightly
In the arms of your commotion,
Absolutely close to you
That is all we need on earth.

There is nothing in the world
Like the closing of eyes in love,
Your beauty is our vanity
And your sleeping next to us
Takes us away from life.

For true love knows no grief
Expects nothing in its joy,
Love has no one motive
Not resenting animation.

Love does not suspect us as
It passes freely through our souls
When often in the faultless dark
We find ourselves beside you,
So let us be more promising.'

Three swans crossed beneath a moon
In gentle morning sky,
The underside of their flight
Turned crimson from the rising sun,
They passed without effort.

A hawk on fire with dawn
Candescent pauses on a tree,
As geese in scarce lines quiver
Across a casual blank air
As if drifting through years.

~ WINDWARD ~

Unnumbered days bow down
Their heads and gentle throats,
Pronouncing a quiet sorrow
Which can never be assuaged
For humanity in distress.

Like a happy bride or girl
Going once with a man,
Or a falcon whose fidelity
Can only ever strike,
Can there be a reflex fate?

Our souls hang in the dust
As if the breeze were frugal,
Motionless we are in time
Without thought or inclination
Toward goodness or love.

Should we believe in sensation
Or the sweet bowl of this world,
A wonderful precious vessel
From which we mutely drink
Till stupefied we desist?

Swallows left us long ago
After the humming-birds departed,
Now cold inflames the forest
Darkness has less mercy and
Last year cannot be reclaimed.

We have misplaced virginity
Optimistic easy loving,
How lenient we were with gifts
Granting each desire its play,
But unlike the birds we have
Forgotten what we should recall.

~ WINDWARD ~

Now once more autumn enters
Our silken auburn calyx,
Damp leaves cling wetly to
The mineral earth in shreds,
Frost decays all fruit fallen
From summer's durable emotion.

Partridge, pigeon, pheasant, quail
The river a black artery,
Autumn like a naked youth
With a silent message bearing
The humid cells of heavy fruit:

Another year's bright adventure
Enters in our core,
Which we - lovers of time
Rejoin and lightly imitate,
Sexual and lubricious
Gorgeously unclothed.

SIX

A PILOT is about to board
Alive, rustling and quivering
With new light and volition
Eyes thoughtless and quiet:

So the universe is disclosed
And we are led homeward,
Through ruddy fields
And archways made of love:

Where the young combine and
Move soundlessly on beds
Of grass and leaves and sunlight,
Genuine as their lips touch.

From their kindness found
Within this embracing,
The depth of all the world
Is reached and justly fathomed.

The darkness makes us shine
With insensible new life,
Paths of iron goodness
Are spotless with vitality:

Essential and without reason
In changing autumn air,
A similitude of tangerine
Apricot and igneous sky.

Where fox and doe together
Sleep in the woods at night,
And a true king at last
Speaks words to the sea.

The bounds are all discarded
Inhibition is unclothed,
Our voyage of new life
Sets out as dawn arrives:

~ WINDWARD ~

On cold watery undulation
Made stainless and silvery,
Lucid in a diminishing sun
As chrome and bronze refire:

To isles where the monuments
Are senseless and untimed,
And woodcock and pheasant
Give their colour to the land.

Sentient trees are grieving
An internal fervent mood,
Retouching fruit which has
Not yet fallen to the grass.

Those who admit to nothing
Stand shadowy and still
In unseen woods of truthfulness
That never shed their foliage:

Where a sound of water moves
As it carefully runs on stone
Among elm and pine and willow
And birds translate this song.

They bear the grain whose fluid
Runs through our motive blood,
In pleasurable saline waves
That we cannot understand.

We are only known by
What continually lies beyond,
As we cross between seasons
Seas, lakes, and grey rivers.

Take the wheel now and direct
Us toward what you perceive,
Catch the air for us so
That we might soon rest.

~ WINDWARD ~

An unconflicted prince of lightness
Dressed in every season,
You stand above the world
A figure of unearthly beauty
Patient as the milky way.

Although we are cannot meet you
Be the oarsman of our boat
Mariner who will master us,
Encouraged by your unwilled
Vision that enshrines this earth.

SEVEN

Sun sets on a yellow lake
As evening light is quivering
Upon the shady underside
Of trees beside flat water.

All the grasses suddenly
Turn brassy and translucent,
In this low settling of days
Luminous with serenity.

Red drops of autumn blood
Lie bright upon wet fields,
Oak and ash are edged with citron
And chestnut brittle darkness.

A bordering of leaves begins
Another minus edge appears,
For you must now cross over
Reckless without hesitation.

Is happiness immutable –
Why have you left us here,
As death handles us like beads
Numbering our vanities?

A two-oared boat of love
Whose silhouette so compelling
Sets out crossing water where
The sun is driven like a wind:

Taking with it all the promise
Which your soul respires,
As voices cry from the waves
Plangent and metallic, saying:

'What is running in the air
Solitude, ordeal, or the freeing
Transit from this world of stone,
What shall we now harvest?

~ WINDWARD ~

So many weak circles
Their loving made unbound,
Perhaps the final ruling is
That we must just surrender.

The paradox of beauty is
Nothing stays or remains,
So we desire a scenery
Which none can recall but you.

It is as if we are devoured
By birds with spicy talons,
Perfuming us with disillusion
Deluding us with flagrance.

The freedom of undying
That we knew of yesterday,
Burns like fire beside the lake
On whose shore we were lovers.'

The speakers vanish yet the songs
Stay with us hovering
Beside our poor memory
Too desperate or full of death:

Weeping for that one who learned
The syllables of ancient years,
Observing human frailty
And its internecine curse.

That one has been supplanted
Grabbed by the heel and drawn
Into flamboyant twilight where
Music is the same as speech.

Now we may remember you
Forever in our language,
Which you refined and tempered
Upon a truth of sound received.

~WINDWARD~

Holding us within your hands
We allow ourselves to be poured
As if in offering to the earth
As bleeding spears of trees darken.

Now through what bars or gates
Can a future bridegroom pass,
What nuptial of genius
Marries modesty and music?

The sun renews our daily passion
That is our mortality,
And each day as we refresh
This consciousness of evening
Your genesis of light returns.

EIGHT

    We only glimpsed you in
    Your beauty and your songs,
    Like a slow meteor burning
    In strong light plunging
    Toward a sleeping island.

    Your words and strange loving
    Were the only visible signs,
    For you never gave yourself
    To anyone except through
    Your instrumental art.

    So your ashes fell like stars
    Down to the aquamarine
    Where you remain unclaimed,
    Yet one or two still recall
    How you walked on earth.

    You loved the port exchanges
    The schooners, monkeys and
    Easy drugs refracting life,
    How you cared to sail, knew
    Gaudy women on far-off coasts.

    Out of the universe came sound
    This was you and your music -
    You, the passenger of that way,
    A journey of the human figure
    Without memory or past.

    You lived among worn sculpture
    Of stone and broken ruins
    Where the scripted almond trees
    Blossomed like snow in winter,
    That was your sole paradise.

    In a small courtyard beneath
    A shining bay-tree's shelter,
    Beside a marble lion head
    You sang for us of old wounds,
    Drank narcotic yellow wine.

~WINDWARD~

You never were an old man
Never surrendered like that
To the rocks and ages
Which compose human life,
You knew just one imperative.

You learned of grief and vision
Reached out and deceased
Before anyone caught those words,
We watched as you passed us
Realised you could not stay:

Telling of the beauty that
You held within your heart,
Of the raw perfection you
So thoroughly expressed,
Which caught you in its arms
As you simply gave yourself
Going from this austere world.

NINE

THE cerulean cloth of summer hangs
Immaculate in a perfect sky,
Beyond the spiked gates of autumn
There exists no retrieval now,
When human love and affection
Withdraw from mundane life.

In this cooling chilling time
Of a contracting year
Strong oaks of chrome and umber
Discard their weary armour
As all the birds take flight
Toward a void of empty nil.

So in life our sickles reap
More uselessness than worth,
In a fluency of present days
This slow-tinted time of falling
When rain makes the air occlusive
And leaves drift on a steely river.

Our lust for all futility
Drives us on compelling,
As bronze-edged shadow scythes
More weight of straw than grain
To lie upon the chilling earth.

Both reckless and creative – we
Whose joy is only imperfection,
Play upon this threshing floor
Of time infused with desire
Where seed is now our only vision.

So the season like a dancer
Undresses her fragility,
And dawn from a brooding sun
Is clothed in serum light,
Where trees flare with cadmium
Winter's old inertia lifts
A frequent shining, say:

'One day we shall have gone
Leaning out on broad wings,
Then we shall not turn to look
Staring only at the distance
Mourning for no life.

For the sun – our fastest star
Causes life to pass in haste,
As days and months encircle
And we walk or stand beneath
The breath of this low-templed sky.

Where night like a stone helmet
Covers over brief effect,
And we imagine that we meet
Only by a hand's friction,
By the sense of love kissing.

Now as violet stars vibrate
Sugary and undissolved,
The smoky flare of your nature
Comes to me this season -
Ingenuous truth without end.'

Those who struggle in this world
Never lose their way,
For what we love masters us
And in our mastery endures:

Gone the long unhurtled days
Tall easy-tempered summer,
Pacing in a vocative sky
When life swivels beyond light.

Then the leaves and trees weep
For human durance and ideals,
For the suffering we pretend
Does not exist on earth,
Medium of our being worldly.

TEN

A LIONESS in moonlight
Uncoils her shining tension
Feral, menacing, and lithe
With inward slowness.

A most natural movement
Emotion we all know,
Bringing us the motive
That takes us through time:

The clarity by which she sees
Unique witness that she is
Of our great dismissal,
A neutral spraying of the hours.

Across life and this world
Of unseen thresholds
We lightly pass on our way,
For there is no shore.

So winter casts its old nets
Lets loose its hunting dogs,
Calls upon a changeless sky
A loneliness of being untimed.

A new moon with her consort
Attendant at her feet
Tears upon the atmosphere,
Long infidelity of time.

The many unseen doors
We pass each day
Not noticing our transition,
Trackless on a damp ground.

A lioness without cruelty
Whose sweet breath and mouth
Seduces us with false desire,
Her blood upon our fingertips.

~WINDWARD~

All the fiction of our life
Where we are merely powerless
Is enslaved by what we love,
Like the scintillating stars.

Upon a two-horned altar
Exposed and so consumed
No offering is possible,
This mental desert we exceed.

By nature and by destiny
We lose the reckless principle
Of how to pursue our kind,
An unreal fire burns the sea.

A life without depravity
Both meaningless and lost
That is our great irony,
Dejection is a knowledge.

Between genius and extinction
We are remade like coins,
Vaguely capturing a truth
Beneath a jagged cerise sky:

Revealing our true universe
Without home or decease
Where we do not change,
Both savage and mimetic.

A burning fire engendered
By the lion in our blood,
Forgotten like a stone blade
Or a perfect moral force:

Only our good nature
Makes us cross an ocean
Without oars or sails,
For courage is our vessel and
Love has a single course.

ELEVEN

A WIND groaning all the night
Taking off our souls to where
There is no time nor light
And living breath has gone.

All night the wind and fronts of rain
Noisy, fierce in a vineyard,
Destroying winter's coarse leaves
Leaving fields and woods flooded.

We lay awake the hours listening
To so many spirits leaving,
The mystery of death, like love
Makes strange the inexplicable.

Love like grief has no bound
Being infinite in space always,
Not to be taken in a word
Contrary to the magnetic.

Then the truths appear on earth
Numberless and unconcerned,
Our admiration for their beauty
Possesses a sagacity
Not easily dissuaded.

We accept their kind gestures
And slow creative moment,
As alone and unique
With time as a blatant sheath
We surrender and submit.

The archery of rain
Ferocious and discerning,
Strikes against a mirrored plate
Shot perfectly toward our essence.

The arrow then turns instantly
Where heart and flesh keep time,
And cast beyond the margins
We are without a suffering world.

~WINDWARD~

So we are renewed each day
If we are justly sensitive,
Giving more than we receive
In time that circles and is passing.

As at sea black ships embark
On voyages to other worlds,
Where one boat without a crew
Sails across titanium roads
With no one at the helm and
No one to adjust the sails.

The vessel goes beyond the sea
Never touching any port,
This is a ship of lightness
Intangible and so unheard.

Neither empty nor illusive
Is the cargo in the hold,
Beneath a rain of human souls
Its freight of consciousness
Is taken far from this hard earth,
That is all you might know.

Like hawks that pause above a wood
Or tall grey cranes upon a shore,
Flyers who never ventured south
When trees began to jaundice:

So much impermanence in life
We are devalued every second,
Like a song whose words are lost
We murmur naked melodies.

Unspeaking to the evening
Beauty twanging in the night,
As sunlight lingers on the grass
Winter hides within a shadow.

What is this season of our life
When we walk the lanes weeping,
Mourning for an unknown minute
Before truth was dishonoured?

Then darkness came with late morning
Its soul within its arms,
Profane and nimble sunlight
Was heard going nowhere:

As all the creatures of the world
Were hiding from experience,
There is neither love nor shame
Nor any interval in cycles.

Such raw and craving beings who
Once strolled this land and coast,
Retreating from the universe
The passionate have no place in time.

Begging for some virtue
As their characters appear and plead,
Passive eyes stare in pity
With friendless insistence.

They comprehend no one thing
There is no simple meaning,
In this ignition of the world
All nature is alight, retreating.

So what is it we need to harvest
Now as the sun retreats,
As curt minor light falls down
Its clean presence gone away
Without inclination?

Friendship is nowhere reaped
Words are exchanged like stone,
What we now endure
Just like the trees in winter
Is the silence of disjection.

The great ovals of the sky
Sweep through us in waves
Of iron, rain, or sunlight,
An elemental force that makes
Human life become ungiven.

So what is it we now gather
What grain cannot be wrecked,
As seeds burn on the forest floor
What hawk leaps from the ashes?

How to retrieve so many days
Force which enraptures us,
From so many broken furrows
What music is perpetual?

When shining silvery veins
With their motive stars,
Descend upon bare hours
With a radius of human voices:

So the immutable was kind
When grass sparkled and trees
Shivered with delicious jewels
Of water made into light.

Then were the lovers young
And linked throughout days,
Their desires like young leaves
Sharp as strong knives:

A new shower of songs came
To the world in broad lines,
To sleep upon the careless ground
And speech was not impure:

Where in love girls and youths
Briefly held the earthly wheels,
In their arms after nightfall
When your kingdom returns:

~WINDWARD~

Where soul is being raised up
A perfect crimson sphere,
Immaculate and gleaming
With wet uncaused life.

The flight of a bird
Or measure of a wave,
Beneath a beaked moon
Soundless and trackless
With no earthly trace:

Inevitable and incomplete
Its line of beauty is a curve,
And those who are prepared to go
Shall always be invited
Rubbed clean of their pattern.

TWELVE

The unaging and obdurate sea
Where gracious swan and seal
Drift in the fertile winter,
And whale's breath is unobserved.

No apparition is seen here
For despair is unknown,
Nothing ever recurs for
No word has been spoken.

The kind of sea you would marry
Not for pleasure but for years,
A soft undertone of ocean
Always playing in the distance.

Solemn trees and bent grass
Cover and dress a flat terrain,
Where grouse or coloured snipe
Live without destiny.

There are two fates in the world
One of time, the other - death,
As the human form steps out
From its envelope of beauty.

Where all human metaphor
Is primarily an act of love,
Our first maritime voyage was
When soul crossed these grey waves.

Master of all patience – ocean
Never grievous, never poor,
Lapidary in its strength
Oblivious of destitution:

Deaf, immutable, inarticulate
Yet vivacious and dazzling,
Whose sea-bell and foghorn
Befriend the sloops and ketches.

~ WINDWARD ~

The hard cold vertebrae of winter
Discarded from the sea to rest
On these poor wet sands where
Gulls scream toward the dusk.

Birds cry as the sun reflames
Low pink bars of morning,
The slow dialect of time
And sensual stress of earthly life.

If sacrifice creates duration
Allowing us to view our source,
Like deer among the oak trees
Who bring us passing joy:

We must never compromise ideals
Nor outwardly deny them form,
But hover in that spaciousness
Between quietness and belief.

Marriage of marine-pastoral
Of curtained beds within houses,
Shells and stones of ancient lives
Iron fragments in the grain:

The small brown cattle of this island
Sheep and crows in the dew,
Long stretches of yellow twilight
Among trees and standing shadow:

Engines beating in the darkness
Of glaucous phosphoros offshore,
Curling repetition of the swell
Susurrus of slow-drifting stars.

They came as soft white petals
Untouchable and implicit,
Unseen vessels of transient hours
Bearing cargoes of invisible life:

~WINDWARD~

Their icy naked exposure
Loving what is without cause,
Sometimes we heard those motors
During long unmentioned night.

There is no foretelling love
No premonition nor defrayal,
For timeless and obdurate is
The experience of worldly suffering,
Of human victory craving vision.

THIRTEEN

Dawn upon grey mountains
Whilst in the valleys – shade
Holds an inner darkness close
Upon a pathless ground.

A tissue of hard bleak ice
Seals ponds from the sky,
A glassy film where we succumb
To bloodless cold oblivion.

Thin white shapes within a forest
Receive the crimson radiance,
As diagonal and slanting cloud
Glide above an amber summit.

A visionary breathless owl
Among powdery conifers,
A small fox treads on stone
As candid birch sway and bend.

Wraiths of snow turn quietly
Unaware of human life,
Their smooth hairless winter body
Colourless and opaque.

There is a moral light on earth
Where the silence of compassion
Shines and gleams and assumes
Us when we are most still:

Beyond all the highest birds
In places where no life inhabits,
Away from the careful deer
From any possible track:

No breath goes upon that air
A dense grey glare subdues
All being within its field,
Not one tree bears movement.

In solitude we find ourselves
Where the genius of kind
Exposes and observes our weakness
Admires our desperation:

The desolation we require
Which like sunlight defines
How it is necessity
Acquires one simple force.

There, having made our way
Alone we are restored,
Taken up by verbless forms
In benign renovation.

The universe extends its hands
Its fingers explore our heart,
Testing the misery and sorrow
Aspiration that made us strong.

Justified, we are admitted
Our lives repossessed,
By horned and intransitive
Gestures we cannot see.

What causes foresight to be true
Drawing us toward beauty,
When lives of certain artifice
Accomplish less than we know?

Like the frailty of snow
Shaken from pine needles,
Or music made upon a bone
Composing us with melody:

How animal we are in life
Compelled in so many ways,
Affection only vivifies
Our brief extent of time.

~ Windward ~

What combustion in the soul
Sustains this living we pursue,
What leads a soul to issue
Upon a midnight bed of passion?

Born as creatures we
Are formed by the vivid sun,
To create and recreate
A world of transparency
Where life does not part with love.

FOURTEEN

The universe is more dark than light
Colder than it is warm
More hidden than any stone,
Intimacy and fierceness of love:

Where radiance is the origin
Source of our many deaths,
And sorrow and regret are
Cancelled by brief excitement.

On the sea light hovers
Like an unseen bird looking
Down for shells within the waves,
A perpetual bluish flashing.

Fragments of broken pine
Dry and smoothed by water
Litter a coarse and sandy earth
Where trees reach to the shore.

Cold azure of the distance
A currency of discreet life,
The concentric world we draw
Towards us in our vision:

We walk among brown rocks
Watch the heavenly sky for hours,
The king and queen of life
Joined in aerial marriage.

A din of feckless days
More unearthly than we know,
As the rounding wheel of time
Circles the memorial stones:

More durable than experience
Greater than human suffering,
Fixed as those stones we wait
Like water made of light.

As flames of human soul
Soft envelope of life,
We pretend to know and love
Then expire without effect
As the world rolls on in space.

So what is love's use, say
What is it that compels,
An old ghostly imperative
Which never lets us rest?

Hovering and whispering
About our words and doing,
Never allowing us to pause
Or be without endeavour:

Love makes a pavilion of us
Candle and perfect font,
Without us love would not move
The breath hidden in life.

Not permitted to stay
Driven like a flock we are,
As if closely herded
Then casually superceded.

Used and so discarded
We are the tread of love,
Footprints upon powdery dust
Quickly a scarce impression.

Sometimes a small quiet door
Opens in the universe as
Love's being strips and proves
The beauty of its torso.

Yet subtle limbs remain hidden
Showing off no passion,
Humanity finds terminus
In corridors that are unknown.

~WINDWARD~

What is love's use, say
Or can we not express
One overt word telling
Of this purely secret visage?

Beyond an adventitious sun
More than any warm spirit
Unaware of grief's force
Doubtless and immeasurable:

As snow falls upon the sea
We are lightly touched,
For love imposes courage
In slowly making us submit,
Radiant and sovereign.

FIFTEEN

This wheel on which we are thrown
Balance where we are appraised,
Slow tribunal of a life
Beautiful as a star.

'What is your name', says the wind,
As icy dust blows tassels of snow
Frozen mauve with light, super-cold
Miraculous with mastery.

It is not the trial nor solitude
But the waiting which is an ordeal,
Where we stand alert in
Cadmium, vermilion, topaz dawn.

For who has seen the little hours
When snow falls before our eyes,
In emptiness and literal silence
Its capsule of a soul alight?

As we attend the patrols of those
Passing printless and unseen,
Exposing their gravity
And transparency of kind:

If all of life is an impulse
To form in a universe of void,
What is it we have conceived
Which no one else observes?

We fall in love on earth with beauty
And what more can we say,
Must we put aside our vision
If we surrender to adore,
Is that the justice of the world?

Now here on this impervious shore
Wind and water mixed with light
Where all of time is suddenly freed,
Human knowledge is released
Experience loosed from its frame:

This issue come from zero
Where clear salt in sprays
Sparkles through fresh blue air,
Our being reconciled with love
Gently inhabits the emptiness.

We hear voices no one knows
See figures who do not exist,
In purely abstract music they
Dance on arctic green water,
Ankles like pink dawn.

Far out there are sails bending
Souls gliding through absent space
Inspecting this terrestrial coast,
Unaware that we observe them
Immaculate they are and perfect.

Where quick gulls and terns inscribe
In white script a subtle breeze,
A language so refined and rare
Humanity has forgotten the words
Telling of life not immediate.

Many ships of past centuries
Touch upon this present landing
Where mariners and their women paused,
For love has caught them in a net
Made blood separate then rejoin.

At midwinter's partial zenith
When the years fall downward,
We recreate ourselves, grow old,
Die - as one or two
Are witnessing this cosmic body.

A woman's eyes of indigo
Of tortoise-shell ambiguity
Beautiful as a galaxy,
Watching her hero, wondering
If she gives herself – how will he fail?

Windward

Pines, cedars, weed, shells
Naked youths upon the sand,
How their leonine beauty shines
Smooth, faultless and desiring
Without need for honesty.

Their love is a complete medium
Unmoving, fully sensitive,
A palpable gulf of tactile music
Where breath passes in syllables
Received from lip to mouth.

The lean ocean is possessed
By its memory of human lives,
The vibrance, odour, and suffering
Of those who travelled its surge
Currents and vast oblivion:

Migrants and voyagers keen
With cargoes of young animals,
Sailors whose love on earth
Could not equal their solitude
Or those fleeing from too much misery.

Fishermen who launched at twilight
Into unlit gales and calms,
Pretending as they throw out lines
That they gather food from depths
Conscious of a phantom world.

Diamond air, grey swells, brown pebbles
Yellow wintry detritus blowing,
White birds cutting the sun's atoms
And hidden blood that is engorged
Where the male and feminine meet:

As the shadow of a fish through water
Or a bird flying at night,
The living soul brings us toward
Correspondence that is vivacious:

~WINDWARD~

Betrayal of all time
Flair and vitality of millennia,
Hovering above this perpetual beach
Where moral thirst is imperative.

A nude body dried by sunlight
Swims the polished sea,
Translucent in the water, going
From life to life and further, saying:

'Look, stranger, all around
Not everyone halts at the finishing-line,
My love for you is here inclined
These words go further than you know
Yet you will never greet me.'

SIXTEEN

On this rare earth where we wander
The driven years like particles,
Until unfailing life appears
To take us on in time,
Slaves copulating in the dark.

Icicles and snow surround us
Broken rinds of floe,
Obscurity adheres with deathly
And intimate confinement.

So we walk gazing upward
Across the stone bridges,
Low arches where our souls
Simply over-reach themselves:

Looking down for indication
Tracks or marks showing
Where another being once
Passed across this stark world.

A hawk upon a wire enthralled
By all that it observes below,
Few birds survive this night
Breathless without recital.

If life is fashioned out of water
There is no single fragrance here,
Aquamarine the sky and summit
Are tinted only with a promise.

A great indifference surrounds
Each tawny springing dawn,
Somewhere beneath the whiteness
A golden root awaits:

Beauty of a human nucleus
Throughout changeless days,
Unclothed, unbearable, and pointless
Skimming through the universe:

~WINDWARD~

I reared a falcon in my mind
Handsome, wild, magnificent,
One morning when the sun appeared
The bird flew as I was sleeping.

So I renounced all love in life
Lived apart in many ways,
Loaded with fiery apprehension
The falcon had been my all-the-world.

Wind, trees, light itself
I watched and waited for the bird,
Yet hovering time passed on and
The earth became a vacant place.

Until I realised that this life
Was nothing but the falcon's vision,
As every russet dawn glanced down
The bird returned invisibly.

Now on hilltops all is quiet
As someone holding up a mirror
Stands behind the sky and
Appears to us in perfect silence.

So who is that gold-eyed wanderer
The wordless traveller who
Has no stories which to offer,
Telling of no visions that
He received whilst enduring?

We circulate and dance as if
Music was not unheard,
The footsteps and the rhythms
Of which travellers tell
When they turn homeward.

The journey of the blood and
Its continual measuring,
The speed by which the sun
Rises up to us each morning:

~ WINDWARD ~

Time steeping us in pollen
Redolent of unearthly joy
The love which makes us wait,
All this the wanderer says:

'Among the rocks and strong light
Staring at the iodine sea,
Listening to the old-young voices
No longer present on earth:

There among hard dry stones
Mineral desiccated hills,
Out upon a narrow cape
Above a sparkling ultramarine:

A rhythm and a music of
Engines passing in the dark,
Of unworldly motors bringing
Movement to a signless place.

There are white birds in the trees
Enjoying venal fruit,
They sing and play, performing
Before our tangible vision.

Ships pass beneath us calling
As we ascend the sky,
Assumed by clear transparence
A lucid envelope and sphere.

They cry for us to ring the bells
To acknowledge their departure,
The young in love are captured
By the sweet warmth of voyaging.

Brazen life is so removed
From a flood of senses touching,
Where humanity was caught and bound
Upon a weaving of desire.

~WINDWARD~

For we bear experience quietly
Waiting for a day when
We cease to be fallible and
Ordeals are just light.

It is greatness that makes doors
In the moral genial sky,
Until we leave our souls at last
Like garlands on a terrace,
Faithless like winter, inert.'

SEVENTEEN

LOOKING at your eyes is where
We always want to be in time,
Magician of pursuit, you
Are the knowledge we assume.

Arising out of nothing you
Are the one who makes us true,
Appealing to you we become
Caught in a trance of love.

For there exists one story
One undisclosed book,
In this world of practice
And long human effort.

We wept for the old year
When in the woods at dusk
We came across its charcoal
And twigs from a lonely fire:

A skull uncovered during winter
In a forest on a stone,
How many of our days are passed
In waiting for affection?

We wept for manumission
From this transparent universe,
Animating what we do not say
As we crave your image.

A cold grey north wind
Ran across the sandstone lake,
Thin sharp waves drove toward
A shore we could not recognise.

Geese were crying somewhere
In a low colourless dusk,
As they fled away from us
The old year quietly vanished.

~ WINDWARD ~

Dawn seemed late the next day
Touching first the tops of trees,
Softening the grass and earth
Making birds appear golden.

Once again with our cargo
Of anxiety and solitude,
We prepared the boats and rigging
The thin sails and worn steering.

How is it that we master
So much oblivion in time,
How is it to live disguised
Deceived by our own amity?

We hid our tears and sang
Of how sorrow had given us
So much in this open world,
What we lost we barely knew:

Love, truth, the pleasing scent
Of another intimate soul,
The warmth of another's body
Pleading for simple kindness:

The efforts and the endeavour
Years, walls, songs,
Shirts we wore and exchanged
Rooms of portraits where we waited:

Courtyards, gardens, friends
Youth, marriages, uneasy lives,
The empty houses, silence
And reticence of old travellers.

There are shadows in the new light
Children, infants, girls,
Places where we might watch
Quiet pictures proposing life:

~ WINDWARD ~

The bravery or ambition of
Companions who had yielded,
Landscapes where love was
Unaware of more than nature.

That is the bright sanctuary
Where from nothing we become
Visionary and solitaire,
Aware of your existence we
Can go further than we know.

EIGHTEEN

It is that dismal time of the year
When death mates with life,
From the stiff ground appear
Small green arrows of fertility
Hard spears of earth's passion.

Our life is doubtful till
The sun of justice speaks,
Measureless with shadow
Fashioning the seeds
In long and disquieting dark.

As we supercede ourselves
Little remains of each minute,
Fugitive and inconstant
In this boundless universe
Where love is secret and an art.

White roads gleam with salt
The river breaking black with ice,
The sky a transcendent rouge
Where life is dazzled, changed
To cold superlative light.

Rims of stone turn endlessly
Making grain of soft dust,
Spring unsheathes from winter
Streaming over stones and rocks
Evaporating grey frost.

Now the year puts on a diadem
Of snowdrops and of crocus,
White and gold and purple buds
Upon a brow of warm bronze
Of radiant loveliness.

Our corporeal emptiness
Renews a gradual vibration,
Compelling and impulsive with
The tension of fresh life,
Cold dark rain falls at night.

~ WINDWARD ~

The earth receives a guest
We put aside our grief and
Prepare to dance for marriage,
With a crown of young birds
Singing in the laughing trees.

So we go back and forth
Oscillate in gentle waves,
Once more the rites commence
Making drops of blood fall
On incidental time.

A turquoise sea is flashing
The first small sails appear,
The mercury of new dawn
Pours out its lust upon
A startling aquamarine.

This is the golden root
Tongue of single words,
Unseen fire that needs to heat
The random fluid of desire
Where conception is informed.

Men and women retrieve joy
As they closely rise from sleep,
Out of darkness so renewed
The world assumes a bridal dress,
A universal wedding gift
Of flowers in a perfect ring.

NINETEEN

Travellers can never return
To places of perfection,
And those who go weeping
A cup of mere grain within
Their unbarred private heart,
Endued, they are, one day with
Smooth fields of green wheat.

Such is time's mobility
The various bones of a skull,
Where three expressions tell us
Of death's weightless threshold,
Its broad white gateway
Guarded by two patrolling swans.

First, a weakening of strength
A creaking of the vessel as
Sinew and illusion relent,
Then the weariness of loving
Always surrendering our souls
Knowing we cannot be met,
And finally the quiet admission
That we cannot lightly triumph
That victory too is one day closed.

Ineptitude of mindless youth
Struggles of maturity and
Stillness come of slow age,
And yet more durable than these
Or any stone or hard element
More firm than even old songs:

Paradise is always open
Always turned toward us,
Waiting in the near distance
Both immediate and remote,
In the ideas we must perfect
Ideals that reveal those doors
Made pure by being invisible.

~ WINDWARD ~

Paradise receives our bodies
The useless breath we spoke
Telling of inconsequence,
Even for the unclothed lovers
Apprehensive with their bias,
The beauty of joined nakedness
And those simple words.

Only travellers tread paradise
For if we never move our ways
We are not transformed,
In the transit of a human soul
Is more than the world can found,
More than even gravity which
Supplies our sensory wealth:

The grasses and the leaves
The timber for our voyages
Children of the future
And how we tell them of our kind,
Liberal fields we might describe
Where white birds stand guard
And the journey has no motive.

TWENTY

Consume me now, great with passion
Fastened to another day,
And listen to the hammering
Neither bird nor human,
For there is a globe
Enclosing us within this world.

New light comes flashing
Glassy with clear vigour,
As earthly life renews its being
Its embryo revived:

Perhaps to stare upon seclusion
Where loneliness can triumph,
With eyes and with a soul that
No one has conceived or seen.

What to do when all is done
And the seeds are folded in,
Laid among bleached leaves
Stored in the cool future:

When the lions of our vision
Pace away and leave us pausing
Beneath the casual form of trees
And the fields are calmly sleeping?

What to do when fulfilled
And the surplus days run out,
When still green shoots arise
And lilac-purple bulbs shine?

Nervous and promising with love
Drops of moisture fall at night,
As darkness grips us close
And the wanton grain is heavy
Unseen and unknown.

Then comes a snowdrop, hidden
By broken ice and rotten snow,
And with newly-angled dawn
The modest crocus shows herself,
Small, bold, and all-renewing
Signal spirit of another world.

The riches of the hyacinth
Stare openly on earth,
The tall phallos of the sulphur
Daffodil uprears itself
To sway in cool damp vernal air.

These are the souls who walk
Through light and time with beauty,
Creative and inspiring us
Till we displace our shadow
And futile indirection:

Light-hungry creators who
Struggle in their way toward
New pictures of the juvenescent
Drama of a human-kind.

Oil of light, they are now
Inscrutable in loving,
Who bring us to our freedom
And visions of no place.

Unbound and slightly going
They make us more truthful,
Leading us like autumn leaves
That went down before winter.

To this rippling slow conception
Of the purely sparkling dark,
Messengers, at first hesitant
Arrived, to enter one by one:

~WINDWARD~

Ruthless and yet hesitant
Shy at first then strong,
Moving far within our bodies
Disciplined yet stray in love:

Never idling in their pleasure
Nor disappointed by response,
Further in our bloodstream they
Through suave curtains gave themselves.

The messengers then departed
Like instruments replaced,
Back to darkness smiling
Fecundity and flood withdrawn.

This engraving of all life
Upon our fertile moments,
A cyanine dye within our soul
As caught in a ring we are
Left alone in solitude and
Arrested by the voyage.

TWENTY ONE

Who is that in the sky
Silent, introspective yet
Passing above our presence
Wordless and untouchable,
Drawing us to another world?

What blood is that streaming
Upon cumulus and cirrus
On flaming antlers of vermilion,
Humility and beauty spiked
With gorgeous fissured texture?

A last white frost upon the grass
Like fresh untrodden ashes,
Unprinted and delicate where
The risen sun strikes a path
Of richness to new days.

It is only lovers who perceive
This ultra-flash of joy,
As it rears out of the east when
Together they fall asleep
In envelopes exceeding time.

So the quiet archer draws
Human souls from death,
Uncalled and unhurried going
Through unworldly grey doors
Crossing from life to life.

Yellow wild forsythia flares
Upon the brown hedges,
And fine candid pear trees
Blossom beside black roads
As if celebrating marriage.

Swans and geese come home
So enjoined by fresh light,
Unbounded now and free
Of the ordeal winter makes,
A necklace of morality.

They unweave the dark - this
Imperfection of our being,
Pitiless, guiltless, flawless
They dance with terrific lust
That is profoundly versatile.

A pigeon at a pool of water
Sparrows bathing in soft dust,
Creatures like birds and yet
Touching the wet throat of space
And bloodiness of heaven.

The slowness of sheer gold in grass
As strong years tower overhead,
Their supernal rule impelling
A play of running streams,
The river drifts unnoticed.

Upon the horns of atmosphere
Unseen doves and starlings cry
Like ghosts in search of destiny,
A low and sacred radiance
Pours out a quick currency.

So the spirit carefully wanders
Robust, invincible, insistent,
A silver being made discreet
Whose messengers crowd around
Invisible, imaginary.

Upon a flat lake the sun
Reclines upon a citrus sheet,
Within a tall dry forest
Illuminous and motionless
Love is gently loosened:

Children's voices in a woodland
Grains of light infusing shadow,
Whilst beneath a crimson arch
Above us souls gather and
Disguising their compassion
Weep for humanity.

TWENTY TWO

The makers of the universe
Elegant and wild appear
And offer to the devoted
Their kind state, saying:

'This veil made of human tissue
Grey diaphragm of damp light,
Is drawn aside like a screen
In moments of great love.'

Then once seduced - the memory
Lives by day and season,
As lovers are swept onward
Towards creation and decease.

Without love there is no grief
Mourning is our brief renewal,
The beloved has departed and
The void of life become exposed.

An old man drifting into sleep
From which he will not waken,
The lovely swan within his pulse
Has taken flight away.

Regardless of where we walk
Or how our travels circulate,
Our duration on this earth
Is fixed and firmly bordered.

The only journey that is worthy
Is when the human flame
Perceives its bright sentinels
Numinous without haste.

It is their causeless presence which
Brings us to assurance,
Removing all remorse as
They explore our moral heart.

~WINDWARD~

There is no action except speech
Language is our only doing,
The perfection of a word
Is all we achieve in time.

A gift of silence or
Offering of consideration
Brings more to this earthen world
Than any feckless substance:

Where blood and humid issue
Are poured out and reformed,
We see with our eyelids down
We are just what we say.

Like cormorants in the rain
Or almond blossom falling
Upon the nests of brooding geese
The light makes us indefinite.

We had our premonition
The supernatural voices,
To tell us of our mystery
Of fidelity and fluence:

Small hyacinths in a sapphire ring
Whiteness of young apple boughs,
A penetration of new worlds
Of the moving sun and stars.

A cold pang of wet dew
From off sharp bamboo-grass,
Out of winter's infinite
The earth is now impressed.

A nightingale all night
Singing through the darkness,
Repeating to the sultry trees
The ardent secrecy of spring
With lightly passing stress.

~ WINDWARD ~

Those who only dwell in light
Who visit us in time,
Captivate by plea the earth
With urgency unspeakable.

The irony of life is that
They who lose themselves in love
In admiration for the beautiful -
They only give themselves away.

So goslings on the river hide
At noon among the reeds,
As coots and teal swim
Upon slow-flowing streams.

These days of elevated light
White dogwood now in flower,
Delicacy of leaves and birds
Of small shadows on the grass:

The innocence of rainfall or
Coition before dawn,
When closed doors and windows
Refrain the stillness of the night.

Then vision is a place apart
We knew it well but never paused,
As once beneath the chestnut trees
We gave away our birth.

Now is a time to plant trees
For saplings to be cared for,
So we might recall the season
All that was hidden in the world
When the lovers fell apart:

That perfect order of the creation
When spring is constant,
With true light and true sky
And belief - its first stars
Where we cease to die.

TWENTY THREE

Lilac and wysteria days
In the dogwood stilling light,
Chestnuts raise their plumes
As oaks show off ornaments.

Life's indifferent passion
Among this fiction making
Men and women endless
In their pursuit of love.

The beauty of flowering trees,
Whose momentary lightness
Is shining on the bodies
Of men and women as they meet.

In the distance between truth
And presence we pretend
That dueling we are one
Sonorous new beauty.

Unique and mysterious fluid
Unrevealed in the world,
Flooding with dense current
Between the male and feminine:

A text that is at one
With all the years conjoined
In this universe and the sun
Of reason we call our own.

Like the taste of water or
Shadow that is in light,
Perfume of the sky or
Possibility of human joy:

Rain and showery days and
Loneliness of being human,
Desperation we reject
So that we might continue:

~ WINDWARD ~

This our unspoken word
What we never really knew,
Why, how, with whom it is
We are upon this earthen floor.

These serene white days
Blossom and sunlight dancing,
All the tongues now alight
With every natural desire.

Hours that seem to hover
Where slim heron glide,
Insects drifting in the shade
And warm sand beneath our feet.

Stillness, slowness, the pacific
Calm tranquil air above,
Grey receding cloud unnoticed
Proceeding quietly westward.

My longing for you and my love
Upon a thin dry shore,
As you lie there almost naked
Imbibing sun within your blood.

Our affection can reform
That first rare seed of life,
What it is that makes us true
Renewed by the sound of water.

No matter what the world removes
From these small gentle hours,
Without knowing we were both
Absorbed and combined by
Complete supernal love.

TWENTY FOUR

If all experience is an archway
Through which we see
A world where we are not,
Beneath a smooth-cast heaven
Through slim blue trees and shadow:

Across a newly flowing river
Beyond the naked swimmers,
Even further than those fields
There are no witnesses to note
How it is we go.

No one oversees our lives
Or overhears what it is
We say just to ourselves,
How it is we are kind or
What it is we give in love.

There as if motionless
Standing in green-gold light,
Further than that old gateway
The universe awaits us knowing
Examining our heart.

Now begins the fluid season
With its juice and sweet seeds,
Flowing water issues with
Running streams and milky skies,
A spilling of fidelity.

Now young birds recall the songs
Measuring small corners where
Night recedes from amorous dawn,
Where nightingale and pigeon
Remake their old love-sounds.

Golden, stainless, undecaying
Small dense violets unfold,
Shining like the sun they are
Distributed upon the earth
As we are revived by promise.

~ Windward ~

A glittering amoral sea
Envelops this gathering life,
Immediate and tidal
Generative and vivid -
Its young bare appetite.

Cornelian glamour of your eyes
The mauve and porphyry
Of unharvested desire,
Sinuous, agile, leonine
A leopard in your passion:

Changeless and inclusive
You are the weight of air,
Impersonal in every word
Touching our inward flesh
Casual and so fertile.

Where does the unique belong
Perpetual and transient, for
Immutable you are and seem
Adorned with yellow croci
Every instrument of life?

Citron light upon the grass
Germination of the spirit,
The constancy of this event
Where men and women wait
In all possible mystery.

There is no sickle present
The ephemeral and contingent
Undress beneath the sun,
Permanent and beautiful as
A field of brazen wheat:

Slightly shivering and waving
Warmed by the atmosphere,
Bearded, heavy with soft grain
Lightly swaying as if
Apart from mortal time.

Kind and suave is creation
Filling days with affection,
Where soul plunges into space
Issued by the darkness
The joy of being wanton:

Revealing of true light and
Your shining eyes for me,
As you stand beneath an arch
Murmuring unspeakably
Calling out for us to meet.

TWENTY FIVE

Hot nights, saffron evenings
Quartz sun, venous sky,
Afternoons of flags and bells
Pigeons, sparrows, peacocks.

Shadows in the shape of lives
Inhuman and otherworldly,
As dawn with superior eyes
Looks upon our desperation.

Noise of dogs among the trees
A bucket splashing to a well,
Its sound echoing and pausing
A voice calling to a child.

A lone owl perceives this
Waiting in meridian heat,
Where figures move effortless
Unsigned upon the world.

It is as if two surfaces
Sift and in their meeting
A transfer of affection
Draws the psyche beyond life.

Then grief appears on the air
Its thin brown ichor soaking
Livid souls with anguish as
Rain sweeps through paradise.

How desperate we are for meaning
As the rivers drench us slowly,
Remorse at the lonely hours
Inspires us with patience.

We are shells informed by light
Wafer become wet,
Recurrently evasive we
Cross and recross a landscape.

~WINDWARD~

If only truth is admitted
We cannot be alarmed,
Where beauty perfect as a mirror
Lies invisible and naked.

Beneath lavender shadow
Of a tree beside a lake,
We stayed one afternoon
To be away from sun and light.

Before us fish and turtle
Were browsing the green water,
In a broody fuscous sky
Heron and egret glided.

For a few moments that afternoon
As we rested by a wall,
A breeze caught us in its noose
Out of time and sole.

Without those tenseless minutes
We possess no life on earth,
And our days exclude us
From their mild and porous state.

Beneath that fulgent tree leaning
Out across a quiet lake,
In our vision we were captured
By the beautiful-elusive.

That night the sea was raving
Unfolding on a far shore,
All the hours a flood of rain
Hissed and spattered in the groves.

There were leopards in the midnight
Their zeal and their ardour
Were for human-kind to pause
Become impartial in its loving.

~ Windward ~

For the rites of happiness
Dwelling in the ruling sky
Are never truly evident
Unless our aim be true.

High up in the hills amid
Slow mist and wet vapour,
Remote and secluded we
Crouched beside a cold fire:

Humidity and days of smoke
As thick warm rain softened
The luteus earth by running
In shallow pools of damp sand.

For shade is life on earth
And rainfall its blood,
And time will only move in time
With a silence of minerals:

Where we see with eyes closed
All primaeval space,
A dark pluperfect where
The issue of a soul is free.

As ships pass along the coast
Pressing throughout turbulence,
Hills become indistinct
Hidden by a milky fog.

Then the sovereigns emerge
Within our sparse world,
Revealing a rare transience
Supernatural throughout space.

Briefly with compassion
They offer us their gifts,
Bringing to our pursuit
Signs of intimation:

~WINDWARD~

Within those small instants
Gravity and time recede,
Deathless in their nakedness
They admit us to their company.

One day without compulsion
Without dubiety or pain,
We are clothed and surrounded
Veracity is undressed.

One little day in time
We are opened and exposed,
Where souls are soft and dry
And transparency achieved.

Our anxiety is discharged
As the heart becomes delicious,
Crucial, without momentum
When even love has no force.

We forget what we experienced
When the rains paused,
Yet that one great day inhabits
All the rest of time.

Between creation and annihilation
Stands this one pure season,
Full of sparks, indifferent
Relentless and implacable.

Formal and influential
Life assumes a new attire,
Fresh grasses touch the air
We are reckless and supple.

Impulsive they are and present
Standing in the doorways,
Resolute, unspeaking and
Unearthly in their kind.

~ WINDWARD ~

They do not know their own names
Yet sometimes their suffering
Releases our awareness from
The despond of this place.

Their virginity and lightness
Their joy for us so firm,
Is beautiful and generous as
They reflect a charge upon us.

Apart from all recession
Beyond possible harvest,
Fugitive and aimless years
Run away beneath our feet:

Across a hidden threshold
Where we become companionless,
Hovering upon verdant fields
We enter to their minus-light.

Like a woman's shadow in the hills
Fluent, strong in its pace,
A small liquid star exploding
Burning throughout vacance,
A thin white wake of sudden pleasure:

An iridescent human soul
A bird of turquoise-blue alighting
Upon a flawless tree whose limbs
Are vast enough to give illusion
That this is the only world.

Inscrutable and undestined
Enduring darkness in the world,
Their anguish at this earthly void
Illuminates our being - then
One day they are gone and
We recall their benison.

TWENTY SIX

The mystery of sorrow and
Consciousness of private joy,
We pretend there are no wounds
So we might love more fully
The rites of this living.

Two souls upon a sand shore
Blue lake water at their feet,
And all of light suddenly
Gracious and invisible
As it flows and covers them.

The years and so much error
Small griefs not yet forgotten,
Love that was never said
In profound inner silence
Luminous with passion.

Life arcs overhead
Like an ardent lover causing
The world below to close
Its eyes with pauseless pleasure,
The strangeness of distress, saying:

'I have two souls my love and I
Who keep with me through time,
Both are still and know I am
Dressed only in bare clothing
Woven of their beauty.

Years are closely gathered here
Bend their necks in submission,
All their lives stay and watch
As day sings and darkness weeps,
Hours run away unnoticed.

My soul and I meet each dawn
Vanishing so lightly,
Breathless and unseeing we
Receive the beautiful
Transparence of the worldly.

Where light makes no incision
This being the only kingdom,
We are two souls in one
Who sustain their distinction,
Such is the mystery of love's
Universal promise.

Not death nor phantasy nor life
Nor absolute dismissal
Can fracture that peace now
Where we are joined by ritual
Founded on humility.

I have tried by all means
To be free of the years,
From words and their bodies
That captivate as lightly
As bronze midsummer grass:

So I place these my breaths
In your hand like this,
Loving your exception
Candid and unconcealed
Its validity unsaid.

A cruciform sun arising
From saturating fog
Catches us in a circle
With yellow serum light,
Revealed and justly naked:

The ring a groom prepares
To be given for a bride,
For no death nor any living
Can remove from this present
What was made without sorrow.'

TWENTY SEVEN

There is a golden envelope
Which sealed we convey,
Close within our lives and
Hidden by leaves and stone:

Patterns of the universe
Covered over in our blood,
Story of this moving world
Of sun, moon, and starry hair.

It is the hiding place of all
Our strength and private source,
The beauty we transmit
Making us immune to death:

Arterial-red of hope
Made strong by disappointment,
Ingenious, enigmatic so
Resilient is happiness.

Covered in a fog before
The wind moved one morning,
An island off the coast appeared
Unobserved except by birds:

Crows who praise the day
Eagles whose tall overview
Looks down upon sharp hawks
The passage-way of doves.

All night the sound of rain
Falling on quicksilver waves,
Our lives are like that music
Of a river passing over rocks.

In the reflow of a grey tide
As currents flux and fall,
Sailing boats and fish pursue
Careless roads and stations.

~ WINDWARD ~

Between a mercury sea
And tireless white zenith,
In our soul we set out
Toward a truth we knew.

We do not see how time
Is running faster than we go,
Except for those fractions
When lightness changes us.

Then as moral creatures
We recognise ourselves, saying,
'Virtue cannot perish nor
Can the slowness of pity:

Paradox of men and women
Or the mystery of death,
In this ultimatum there
Is nothing to be spoken.'

All our strangeness like a curtain
In the tawny light of evening,
Quietly parts to reveal
Inhuman figures always passing.

At dawn the sky is fully lit
With coloured flashing fire,
The flare and shot of life
Expressed upon our vision.

The youthful blonde of summer
Your hand touched my hair,
Being true is our only measure
Essential and courageous:

A gentle liberal gesture
Securing one experience in
Broad days beneath the sun
Where the beautiful is hovering.

~WINDWARD~

What love for a blade is there
Or commanding wheels,
Where rhyme is ubiquitous -
A further null-point?

Beauty lies in retrospect
Lightness we fairly inhabit,
Yearning for tangible life -
Reticent days without temper.

An ivory ring is open now
The issue made, a circle broken,
Time ends by sowing joy -
We await the messengers.

They will unloose the secret
Which we have so endured,
Suffering shall be removed and
The pain of being stripped
To shining freedom.

TWENTY EIGHT

Between truth and untruth
Walks a casual wanderer,
Between breath and stone
Carnal water floods.

As we take the veil that
Caught us like a cloth,
We take it to shield from light
A milky universe within:

Superficial membrane and
What cannot be known on earth,
Awful and terrific love
Between certitude and nil.

One shining figure stands
Between years and the rest,
In sleep where we stroll
Beside slight black trees:

On the stone edge of a shore
Fresh lake water or waves,
Mild grey stream in our soul
Fluid of unspeakable treasure:

Between nothing and one
Are the new lovers avowing,
And all the young guests
The land, its mammals and snakes.

Nude with each other
Revealed and so bare,
Being removed from life
Now joined by this savour:

Unbearable sweet cavity where
A river flows from our tongue,
Our innermost compulsion
Coursing without thirst.

~ WINDWARD ~

Between girl and boy and
The beauty of a human face,
Is all that we have endured
Between honesty and doubt:

The lost dancers pause
To look about themselves, amazing
At the farewells of men and women
Their mercurial affinity.

Like an oar dipped to a river
Or two swallows dashing briefly,
Flashing a white curve
Through the humid air of June:

Making us vivacious
Driving us insensible,
Between death and experience
Like a bowl of fine sand:

Grain in the human core
Gravid no longer,
We remember the deserted
Motive of impassioned heat:

Dry hill-tops where we waited
In order to be renewed,
Undressed from coercion
Stripped of anatomy.

Between these moments
A murmur does not pause,
A mask hides us from ourselves
In apertures of singing flame.

So we take this veil of speech
Admire what we are losing now,
Emptied of every craving
Anointing each other's eyes
Marrying dust and pleasure.

TWENTY NINE

Days when we sailed for joy
Past heron and cormorant rocks,
Deer were swimming out to the isles
As we flew beside them watching.

We had felled our own firm mast
Set it deep and green upon the keel,
Our fires we had brought with us
Conserved upon smooth stones.

Days of harvest and of sunlight
Of quiet anastatic waves,
Like the milk of paradise it seemed
A universe caught in one picture.

Our spontaneous voyage set out
At dawn across the bay where
Yellow pollen covered over
The sea with filmy powder.

Days of watery happiness
With the sound of a fractious wake,
Of shores scented with young pine
Where we slept fearless and easy.

Sailing past remote sea graves
Ancestral marine tombs we knew,
Always wet from spray they were
From waves who loved those sailors.

Days when hours were not wrong
When music was ours to sing,
When we kept our own imperative
And courage was indelible.

The eager spinnaker visible
To all who were navigating,
As if followed by beauty we were
Like a lover and her beloved.

~Windward~

In regions where it never rains
Fully hidden in the light,
Being brighter than the day
Than mundane suffering:

There are guardian helmsmen
Compassionate and pitiful,
Who oversee and direct us
Invisible like sweeping clouds.

Faithful just to shadows they
Are motionless - our boat skimmed
The patient medium of their sea,
An impartial indifferent void.

Midsummer when the fertile sun
Poised in our breathing heart,
Unlocked its truth as we were still
And took us for its own vessel.

Having sipped the water of genius
To be human is to endure,
To receive the unfamiliar
And secure gratification.

We curved like light and shot away
Unconditionally released,
Living for more than ecstasy
Free of this world's diminishing
With an archery of a new life.

THIRTY

Along the prolific seaways
Where we sailed once,
The mutability of affection
Made harvest of our fertility,
So we were always timed.

There is no interval to life
Only the courage to admit
A unique stream where
Humility of love exceeds
All material measure.

Between idea and instant
And the stony pebbles of grief,
Sorrow and necessity are
A long swell breaking open
In strong grey waves.

The sea a colour of ashes
Lavender tinted sky,
Leonine rocks, blue figures
Who patrol the dry silence
Like water becoming rain:

As if ocean's breaking
Was powder heaped on sand,
With a noise of birds' wings
Whose only bliss was coition -
Bird of conceivable space.

Dormant in the loose shade
The bend of day remains
Captious and unprincipled,
Like young lions in zenith heat
As trees quiver with light.

There is a sadness to loving
Someone who is unaware
Of either how to receive
Or how to offer affection,
Luxury of human kindness.

~WINDWARD~

Then over the sea they came
Unstained and yet infinite,
Imperfect but never vain
Source of current and aeon
And all inhuman law:

Driving on through boundless years
To this white shore,
The bringers of optimism
In their grey shivering skin
And gleaming mineral eyes.

Time like a copper stylus
Of silver-beveled lines,
Stainless, evasive, superfluous
Its point perfectly at rest
With liberty and a reflex universe:

Within our sleep we held
The hours of space and coalesced,
Symmetry made us true
Congruent with each other,
Personal solace we could assert.

From despair came moral right
The sanguine artistry
Of creativity and love,
Interlude of child and woman
Between women and their men -
A generation of ideals.

THIRTY ONE

Like fireflies on a summer night
So our nakedness in this world
 Is touched by a river, lake
 Sea, ocean, ulterior clouds
 Rain streaming in threads.

 So too our understanding
 Is circumscribed by being
 Here on a stony earth,
 We are limited by objective
 Caught by our wet blood:

 The void beneath a mask
Where human lust and sorrow
 Are fast and consume
 The naturally beautiful,
Such is our poor dilemma.

 How solitude perplexes us
 The bare extent of time,
 How we struggle in this moral
 Silence of imperfection
For one simple diamond truth.

Chromium coloured and translucent
 The long blue oars of noon
 As boats return and pass us,
 How we crave their meaning
An effulgence beyond thought.

 Undyed we are by daily life
 Untouched by its meteors,
 So much procreation
 Milky waves forever folding
 On a tideless dry shore:

The brackish taste of human love
 Water of our virginity,
 Thorns hidden by the light
 That touch us so casually,
Unbreakable shell of darkness.

~WINDWARD~

Transfigured by affection
Or in the cry of snakes,
As in our stone room sleeping
We re-enact oblivion
Each night as we embrace.

There is a leopard somewhere
Who now and then reveals
Sweetness, happiness and
The causeway of freedom,
But then we always forget.

Yes, we know it there, waiting
Observing our quiet futility,
Like a slow distant thunder
On a lovely afternoon,
Hinting of sudden rainfall
In the unbearable heat.

THIRTY TWO

Like a boat within another hull
In which we oblivious rest,
Unaware of our voyage or
Destination of the bound vessel
Or even of its first launching:

A lioness walks the deck unseen
On the mast a vine springs,
The captain is a captive and
We sail supernaturally,
This is our steering song:

'As the great sun touches its apex
With yellow fingers moving
Sensitive and delicious now,
Light fills our sails and
Time cuts us a passage.

Venus in a pear tree shines
Sparkling and candescent,
Gleaming from the night before
Dawn comes to rinse her hands
Worn by so many aeons.

Heavy foamy flowers of summer
White birds in lime trees,
A weak cerulean sky above
Watery and zinc-coloured,
The tallest poplar shivers:

Fruit is fully low and falling
Goslings test their new flight,
Humming-birds vanish south
As ships depart from port for ever,
From untruth to truth we journey.

Ambition like an anthem or
Unseen gulls crying out,
Like a soul in search of destiny
The sun pours out a path
Always going to windward.

~ WINDWARD ~

Boats return from distant banks
Over curling haline waves
Holds full of writhing life,
Here sunlight is our one gift
No one knows of human terror.

Concealed by green rain we are
Now listening to sirens,
Viewing death through mist
Can we truly dare to love
When instinct makes us vulnerable?'

The ship hurtles softly through
Unmarked seas and voiceless space,
In this first opening of the world
A sound of grieving comes across
The flat calm of morning water.

As cargo-craft pass offshore
Cutting through our jade channel,
Cremation fires glow on a beach
Ashes packed in jars and buried
Wrung with unvoiced sorrow.

Axle chains scream with effort
As mourners compete for victory,
In perfection is our end
Life hidden in another world
Like dinghies sunk in harbour.

We do not know the moving ghost
Running through our veins,
Between the heart and diaphragm
Men and women in one pulse
Of cadence stay united.

On sheets of luminous air
They go back and forth touching,
Gratitude is reversed as
Remorse is conveyed prone
Uncreated for adventure.

THIRTY THREE

On the edge of a sea are birds
Within the waves are rocks,
Islands in the current and
In the distance another coast.

So much have we journeyed
Through galleries of years,
With little water in our hands
There is nothing to be held.

We had our time but lost it
Forsook the fields and hills,
All the groves and orchards
Ancient standing walls.

Mariners call upon the sea
To lead them home from life,
So much imperfection
Indifference of everything.

There is neither ship nor stone
Nor wind nor any movement,
For far inside the blood goes
This slow tide of living.

We must forget completely
Or speak with reserve,
Love is giving more than we know
There are no receipts on earth.

On the coast are white birds
In black night there are sounds
Of an old sea upon the shore
Repeating one or two words:

'I thought you were the sea
As I was building my vessel,
Then setting out I found
You further than horizon.

~ WINDWARD ~

Like an island you were
Or footprint on wet sand,
A young bird gliding
Across the sky's truth.

How long must we await
Before the ship arrives,
Before our complexity
Dissolves in the light?

You were sea and bird
Cautious in the night,
When all creatures sleep
And there are no ideas
I love to touch your hand.'

Even this we cannot grasp
Until the universe appears,
An empty, still, undetected
Being which inhabits us,
So transparently beautiful.

For soon gone to light, we are
Where a sun constantly ploughs
Carving furrows in all we speak,
In our effort to recapture minutes
We reap just a little knowledge.

The argent ring of midsummer
Came down all around,
Whose climax we did not notice
As we bent across the oars
Going far from earthly sight.

The slight reins that control
And order so many lives,
Among the pulleys of the soul
How unbearable and truthful
Is the solitude of experience
And beauty's bounding line.

~ WINDWARD ~

Fire upon an altar flaring
Red lions resting in the sun,
So human intercourse
Drives soul to soul invisibly:

The ocean witnesses our lives
Observing the trials,
How we tolerate loneliness
And the rapine of sleeping.

An eagle was in the air
A doe with her fawn paused
In the bones of a forest
Where another day was rising.

Narrow waves like time itself
Surrounded us remembering,
They knew all experience
Both human and merciless.

Rocks dripping wet with fog
Pine and hemlocks shifting,
An oceanic breeze moved
Blindly upon the land:

Rainy needles are thrown
All night upon the ferns,
Sea-grass and seaweed -
Saturated, soaked and limp.

How the days race past
Like swift birds in flight,
And we barely glimpse them
So undisclosed they are.

As we swam the quick flow
Through celadon cold tide
A current drew us offshore
There was no visible life.

~Windward~

Love had made us navigate
Grey swell and salt blood,
Yet we left no impression
Upon the sea or wind.

Our nakedness in the water
Solitude of the bay itself,
Unlimited and speechless we
Swam beneath that hemisphere:

Touched its quiet hands
Which made us love in time,
The tempo of all motion
So mutually pleasing.

THIRTY FOUR

In high conceptual places where
The origin and demise of life
Are caught and apprehended,
The generous ones appear
As we approach and stare
At their fabulous ambition.

So fame arrives on earth
With arrows and light music,
Saying, 'These are my prophecies
Observe now my undress.'

A falcon through unbroken sky
Knowing well the full mind
Of humanity aspiring,
Comes down on earth to glide
Gleaming in low morning,
Catching and discharging sparks
The sun propels to this world.

A perfect gazing image
Intangible and hovering there,
Without tongue or limbs
It moves completely beautiful
With lucid jeweled-eyes alert.

What sight can frame spaciousness
Where creatures walk and fly,
Where meteors at night like grass
Swerve in transparent waves
Where the falcon stands on air?

The mainstring of her waist
Releases in one gentle touch,
And naked the bird is seen
All her clothing fallen down.

Immaculate and desirable
She causes us to be unclothed,
And we conceive in that place
Unspeakable inward joy.

~WINDWARD~

Like dragonflies upon a lake
Azure and emerald flight,
Hawks now float upon warm air
Herons pause in aqueous shade.

The wheat leans in salient fields
Cattle gather beneath trees,
Tuneful with insects, woods
Are bountiful and sway with life.

Light is powdery, alizarin
A lurid sun poised motionless,
We swim out on the water
Beneath darting swallows.

These soft dustless moments
When grains of incisive black
Hide within the shade
Modest now with demise.

An omniscient flare of sunlight
Makes the river obsidian,
Where a stringent stark aroma
Of lotos sweetens the air.

Kestrels glide carelessly
Swallows think of other lands,
Apples begin to fatten and
Acorns become heavy and low.

'Winter begins in August',
They say, as light collapses,
Lengthens in the pasture as
We are inclined toward
Coolness and the closing
Of shutters and windows.

Young canicular hours
Are no longer innocent,
An imperative vernal love
Has accomplished its desire.

Suddenly the falcon rises
Terse in the light conveying
More than this flush world
Knowing one solitary truth.

Herds are waiting in the meadow
As the bird floats deliberately,
Widely driven on the wind
Looking down upon our life:

This manhood of the year
Womanhood of brief night,
Joined by equivocation
To make each other rest.

Like sparks we are crepuscular
Small flashes of compassion,
Where love dashes between souls
Radiant and instantaneous.

A din of dissolution
Crackles in thick darkness,
Words diminish us unless
Like the falcon our aim is true.

Humility, patience and recession
Are the speed of this good bird,
And silence the instrument
Of its elated flight.

There is no going away from
The severed manners of time,
Rich we are with fullness
Without guilt or one desire,
Universal and so temporary.

THIRTY FIVE

Turtledove of such radiance
Perpetual in all ways,
As we observe your gentleness
Your changes all too soon are gone.

In our efforts to be obvious
Like rain we appear,
Descending we run away
Down paths that are too dry.

There is a grove where fruit
Grows but is ungathered,
Where seeds of virile goodness
Are scattered on the ground.

Only in our slow devotion
Do we perceive that tree,
Whilst you, turtledove, remain
Careless in a green vicinity.

Murmuring in low dawn
The litheness of your wings touching
In restless, delicate air
As scented insects sing at night:

That steep fiction of all life
Irony of our conceiving,
Double truth of kind and
Our infinite evasiveness:

A faithless tenancy of days
Assurance of our emptiness,
Where slightly we come and go
And memories are unfounded.

Like nerves or vivid wires
As years flow away like sand,
Light blurs in the distance
Where birth ties its knots.

~ WINDWARD ~

So our speech is disguised
When we approach your vision,
More closely, less imperfectly
Certain of pre-eminence.

The masks we wear at dawn
To illustrate our solitude,
The manners we assume
And words we cannot say:

The effects of songs, cries
Or mysterious consonants,
Cause us to apprehend
Your verity we barely know.

What is that axiom of rite
If not a man and woman joined,
Their shape locked with happiness
Where every issue is sustained?

Whilst animals are pairing
Upon a weightless membrane,
Like breeze the future moves
More complete than we imagine.

You are for me that marriage
Absolute and combined,
A rarity we cannot touch
But persistently admire.

Then you reveal, turtledove
Translucent and beneficent,
To me, a mariner of love
Who sails far from shore:

Beauty that we cannot hold
The beautiful we cannot name,
Strangely out of time and
Unlike living form.

Turtledove, my soul made more
Undeclared and unsigned,
An agony of loving fully
That is finitely human.

Too light to stay this life
As an evening gone, you are,
Immobile, just as we become
Aware of your bounds.

So graciously you withdraw
To sing before another world,
Soul dripping with delight
Perfumed by the ocean's curve.

Your mastery of sea and music
Measuring the full and sensuous,
The giant stones along the coast
Grinding a repeating surf:

Promiscuous with agitation
Just like the voice of creatures playing,
Intimate but not admired
Each morning when you observe.

All this I know well and keep
Within my heart for life,
Even in the sun's long wake
Running into darkness.

The only truth is my love
For you as sure as heaven,
Deftly moving all creation
With nothing as your tide.

Our speech and songs were water
That we drank and shared,
Able and revived by love
Before death dried our bones.

~ WINDWARD ~

Evening came as the sun
Like a vast and ochre star
Drew up its formal pyramid,
We hauled anchor once again.

That ever-cleansing sea of light
Where nativity began,
Vessel of our being and
All this is yours, turtledove -
Explicitly undone.

THIRTY SIX

What is life but a tense spark
Shot upward from a fire one night
Quickly to a raptor sky.

The call of a snake or
Breath of a passing swallow
Voice of a leopard in the dark.

Sanguine, vibrant, full of suffering
Luminous with promise yet
Always lost in vacant space.

Willing and bearing all desire
Youthful, smooth, then old
Worn by restless despair.

The trail of a shooting star
Sudden bird in an evening sky
Both momentary and lasting.

A young man offering himself
In the eyes of a girl completely
Become the unity of earth.

Lovers in their nakedness
Mourners in a void of grief
Or children as they make a play.

There is no life and no death
In all this tissue of movement
There is one witness in the world.

Beyond form and inspiration
Beyond the chase of any shadow
Stillness and parity of light.

Both denial of humility
And truthfulness of being kind
When no word can be made.

~ WINDWARD ~

Voyage from soul to soul in time
Currency of ten thousand years
Creative and uniquely one.

The scars upon a stone tool
Memory of a humming-bird
As it threads a new nest.

A drop of semen in the blood
The ashes of cremation
The rings in how a tree recalls.

Life is a novel firefly
Born to survive mere days
Flashing in midsummer woods.

An ancient unrecorded sea
Where one just mariner sails
Who is nameless and invisible.

All the rituals we propose
In order to captivate
How it is we pretend to know.

In our walks we are alone
Effaced by a bare terrain
Sure loveliness of landscape.

Only in such quiet footsteps
Might we declare our solitude
The medium of the universe:

When love recedes and we
Retrieve the dust of sorrow
Transparency of virtue.

The temper of indifferent sun
Clothing us with beauty's blood
And courage to exist,
Head of the world – the word.

~WINDWARD~

~ WINDWARD~

POETICS

THERE are four columns of experience surrounding poetry akin to the four dimensions of our mundane and temporal life; upon these our belief is founded. Firstly, there is the world that we all walk through, a landscape of many kinds where people speak and respond. There is also the world that we solely think and feel and which we internally inhabit, the mental and emotional world of an interior view. Then there is the world of visionary reception, a situation that is not really a world but a condition that exceeds anything that we might possibly know, simply on the grounds of its boundless and potential abstraction. Finally, there exists the world of sleep where we occasionally admit to passages of great and active truthfulness. These are the four agencies or aspects of the cosmos and it is from these sources that all our metaphor originates.

The metaphors which compose our experience and thought, our sleeping world and our unmentionable desires and longing, even the secrets that we do not know, all these planes of being that enclose us and arrange the surfaces of what we say, do, or perceive, are the media that float upon an absolute sea, rising and falling to those weightless and immaterial waves.

Sometimes the metaphors combine and join so that they might return and guide others towards what they have conceived. Like rainfall that brings growth to leaves and trees, to the grasses and fields and to all moving life, a metaphor is an act of love, perhaps in fact the primary and therefore most profound act of loving. Time, speech, visual satisfaction, even the sensual carnality of breathing creatures, are all metaphorical in their movement, for such is the nature of actual transition, the impersonal life which surrounds us unspeakably and yet which is constantly exchanging meaning for us here; making us fungible, equalising or staying us in a timely sense of stress.

Our human and mundane love is simply flesh or tissue, the irrefragable *eros* of all our sensation, our ideals and mentality, and in this sense the erotic is the nature of the chronological pattern of an ideal and incarnate year. True love or phenomena lie only in the giving, in the emotionally or intellectually generative, for there is ultimately no reception in fact, not in the world. Love is simply our best medium and ultimately, poetry or any art are merely media, just like mediating prayer: activity that truly takes us away and survives us and also precedes us with the tall pillars of its goodness.

Certain metaphors possess an uncommon strength, an ability to go away and to select their own conclusion. Yet how does such so faultlessly arise and what would make for indecision there, if that were possible? To penetrate such an energy of all force in the cosmos and in such a delicate and effortless manner would be to make apparent the true quality of metaphor; for our *under*-standing of metaphor is what allows us to love and only that powerful surrendering *into* love enables the human psyche or persona to determine its sole and signal departure. This is the only freedom which we might ever possess, a liberty that supplies us with what is in fact the instrumentality or hidden virtue of belief.

Poetry is an action or event that concerns free vision founded upon our four standards. Just as with certain kinds of painting—still-life, landscape, and perhaps portraiture—vision—practical or intellectual—is the sensibility of almost all the metaphors which are engaged by the act of poetry, and ideally a poem is a perfectly lucid sphere that is able to arrest life. There is also the element or dimension of a poem in its sonorous temperament, and the satisfaction generated by that perception of audible measure: or, how it is that the poem approximates to the condition of an old song.

These are the two axes, as it were, of poetry: the extensiveness of metaphor and the profound integrity of how a poem sounds, as the poem becomes limitless and transparent in both fashions. What one perceives in still-life or in ideal landscape is not simply the immobility of the field, but the cosmic moment of that perception: what is in fact—in terms of the poem or the painting—its unique expression as both illusion and as emptiness, and yet the exactly simultaneous experience of the beauty extant and current in what is only and really the ephemeral, where totality or absolution is supplied by the art. Belief is the skeleton or structure of that artistry making the metaphors translucent and insubstantial.

Such comprehensiveness is essentially just one story or one book, one picture or one music, for there exists only one narrative or myth in this world of time and human endurance which we all attempt to apprehend and to imitate in our work. This is the ambition of painters, composers, sculptors, novelists, dramatists, and even perhaps of architects, and this is what poets do in time: how it is that they represent true valence in this living and intrinsically motive and fourfold world. It is the arrangement of metaphor in such works of art that affords us with belief. In true poetry there is no person nor voice but only the sound of a particular vision that has submitted to the laws of expression, to our mortal light of speech. This is too much for our comprehension but not too much for our experience, hence such views are beyond the lively status of any language; for those situations are both intransitive and completely or absolutely informed, and that, morally, is all. There is one text or fabric only in this view, but it is unlike any work that we might know and we might capture it only by approximation: so we attempt to formally approach the outlines of that knowledge and attain to some understanding as to how the images of metaphor are known or transposed onto a temporal plateau. Human love is the single currency of such an activity.

Truth, then, is that unified condition of all experience, ostensibly light, weightless and transparent and without effect. It is the universal substance of all phenomena, both natural and supernatural, and its being inspires life and motivates all the various aspects and bearing of time. Truth is changeless and absolutely inclusive, equivocating between life and death which do not truly occur naturally nor exist in what is only transformation and transition. Ultimately we take a veil as an establishment of our truth, vision which we must hide, and in this sense the veil is proof of what we know: acceptance of a transference apart from time, tissue of sensitive life and its absolute and indestructible veracity. So between truth and untruth we go in time, always struggling and suffering in our lapses, desperate for the oblivion of love, for the infinite brevity of vision.

What an artist sees is not the activity of life but its inaction and immobility, where metaphor serves to present the planes and aspects of that true field. The artist witnesses no instant but only the immensity of human experience captured and relayed, caught and refrained or framed within a conceptual scene. *Art is not life* and one must never confuse these two transactions; art brings the solely unique to life and belief is its invisible lens. There, poetry or song exists in a tradition, in a sequence of great immaterial duration whose origins or source we cannot possibly imagine, but which some do become aware of through their visionary practice and its gradually tempered immediacy – our third column of experience. This is the work of poetry: to know and then to express indestructible and undecaying valence, accomplished, when successful, by how it is that the visible sounds. These are two different sensible axes which we attempt to make convergent, and that intersection, when effective, is an imperishable and pleasing work of art. For the good is equally true and beautiful and the template of belief through which we see, returning us to a fourfold order of this round universe where we cross between envelopes of lucid being, moving from the nil of zero to just one.

There are in this spherical world figures who lightly walk above the surface of the earth, weightless and transparent, who without knowing impart to those who care to attend to their passing a certain vision which admits an honesty that is without imperative. Transformed, without becoming aware of this transmission, what actions remain to those persons who have received such imperishable benison? For their vision is unspeakable and interior and without referent or comparison and thus its force is unknowable; yet without doubt its presence and agency are strangely potent and transformative. Supernature in its being and presence renders timely life ambiguous and ambivalent and this dubiety supplies and sustains a rare pleasure of fulfillment, stabilising acceptance and its momentary realisation, possessing no counterpart nor even counterpoint in human record and the recollection of any time. Those ones who walk this earthly ground, imprinting upon the formal and ideal, the *eikons* who are the real pattern-makers, they are the true figures of speech who certainly inhabit us and who subtly moisten our tongues with their careful and generous manners of affection: their accomplishment effects all that we can vaguely perform here.

I say this because experience has given me what I know and what I know is greater than anything that I can possibly say, even in poetry; and what else exists? In this view there is no place for events: that is the *text* of supernature. There are certain human experiences which exist out of time and which cannot be conveyed by words nor even by sounds and there are images which cohere during such moments but these are essentially not truthful, are *super*-natural in form as mere envelopes transporting the experience. These are individual spiritual bodies that without knowledge or solution and without experience themselves are able to maintain their subtle entirety distinct from other entireties. They do range and move and yet remain apart from any measure. Such beings, invisible and weightless, transfer spiritual passion and spiritual worth.

We sentient and thoughtful creatures however, are materially confined by the syllogism, its mystery and yet its mastery or domination, that strange and unfathomable necessity of the discrete. Only the ideal or idea of genius best indicates the formality of what it means to be free, yet even that condition, by virtue of its perfect compulsion, possesses its own bounds. The experience of the supernatural, being *un*-like any other kind of experience, cannot be explained but only recognised and received. For there do exist beings who do not exist, who are generous and compassionate and fully kind and what they accomplish cannot be known. The supernatural expresses knowledge that is unlike any medium or possession of this world and so its immediacy is absolutely unique. Prayer and its meditation overlook death and it is this quality which supplies the radiance that is impersonal and complete or untimed. It is glorious and good to be free of words or to become soundless without possible effect and to inhabit no one; the finest ecstasy is perhaps to reach forward in order to touch the hand which makes us love.

Truth is thus made apparent and overt by its opening and closing and these are the two locations or stations of truthfulness in our universe. The opening is a plane or fabric, a tissue of infinitely one-dimensional material, informed and inspired by a grey soundless voice, an unlimited and motionless breath which is without substance or outline. The closing is like a great engine without any friction or contact, a motor of immensely unmeasured force, a dynamo that only turns and whose movement is circular or perhaps elliptical; it knows of no stillness, only of slowness. That slowness is to be thoroughly imperceptible and is profoundly inherent throughout all the shadowy display of life or time, the perpetual gestures of becoming where this pulse between opening and closing finds place in the round *choros* of the year, our circular dancing floor. That pulse is the mystery of death or the enigma of male and feminine in their subtle meeting, and these indentations upon a plane are simply two dimensions uniting, being both more and less the same truth.

Truth in this light or sense so becomes four dimensional in its manifest expression. There is initially a distinction that marks the onset of duality or all reason and the nature of discretion; then there is the circulation of the year, that *pneumatic* form which both contains and carries us in temporal transit, the source and origin of all measure. Thirdly, there is the presence of terrain, that ideal landscape where we are founded and which supplies us with our grounding and initial metaphors. Lastly there is the vision of the ideals which cause all the above to emanate in this form. The genius of poetry always proceeds towards an awareness of the absolute potentiality of beauty: this is a force of human consciousness and it is quite natural in the world at large. Ironically, the condition of complete negation is also a ground for the reception of such vital being and there we are actively refined in a fashion of artistry: hence we can lightly say that -
the aim of poetry is true.

Kevin McGRATH was born in southern China in 1951 and was educated in England and Scotland; he has lived and worked in France, Greece, and India. Presently he is an associate of the Department of South Asian Studies and poet in residence at Lowell House, Harvard University. Publications include, *Fame* (1995), *Lioness* (1998), *The Sanskrit Hero* (2004), *Stri* (2009), *Jaya* (2011), *Supernature* (2012), *Eroica* and *Heroic Krsna* (2013), *In the Kacch* (2015), *Raja Yudhisthira* and *Arjuna Pandava* (forthcoming 2016).

www.ingramcontent.com/pod-product-compliance
Lightning Source LLC
Chambersburg PA
CBHW030943090426
42737CB00007B/519